GAME ON!

MADDEN NFL

PAIGE V. POLINSKY

Checkerboard
Library

An Imprint of Abdo Publishing
abdobooks.com

abdobooks.com

Published by Abdo Publishing, a division of ABDO, PO Box 398166, Minneapolis, Minnesota 55439. Copyright © 2020 by Abdo Consulting Group, Inc. International copyrights reserved in all countries. No part of this book may be reproduced in any form without written permission from the publisher. Checkerboard Library™ is a trademark and logo of Abdo Publishing.

Printed in the United States of America, North Mankato, Minnesota
102019
012020

THIS BOOK CONTAINS
RECYCLED MATERIALS

Design: Aruna Rangarajan, Mighty Media, Inc.
Production: Mighty Media, Inc.
Editor: Megan Borgert-Spaniol
Design Elements: Shutterstock Images
Cover Photograph: Mighty Media, Inc.
Interior Photographs: Aaron M. Sprecher/AP Images, p. 27; Anonymous/AP Images, p. 9; Christopher Michel/Flickr, pp. 7, 28 (middle); Don Halvorson, pp. 11, 13, 24, 28 (right); JT Cattelan/Flickr, pp. 5, 20, 21, 23, 25, 28 (left); Peter Cosgrove/AP Images, p. 15; Shutterstock Images, pp. 19, 29; Tony Gutierrez/AP Images, p. 17

Library of Congress Control Number: 2019943202

Publisher's Cataloging-in-Publication Data
Names: Polinsky, Paige V., author.
Title: Madden NFL / by Paige V. Polinsky
Description: Minneapolis, Minnesota : Abdo Publishing, 2020 | Series: Game on! | Includes online resources and index.
Identifiers: ISBN 9781532191664 (lib. bdg.) | ISBN 9781644942819 (pbk.) | ISBN 9781532178399 (ebook)
Subjects: LCSH: Video games--Juvenile literature. | Madden NFL--Juvenile literature. | EA Sports (Firm)--Juvenile literature. | National Football League--Juvenile literature. | Video games and children--Juvenile literature.
Classification: DDC 794.86--dc23

NOTE TO READERS
Video games that depict shooting or other violent acts should be subject to adult discretion and awareness that exposure to such acts may affect players' perceptions of violence in the real world.

CONTENTS

MAD FOR *MADDEN*

Twenty-two pro football players face off on the 10-yard line. Fans cheer under the bright lights of the stadium. This is no Sunday-night broadcast. This is *Madden NFL*!

Madden NFL is a sports **simulation** video game series created by Electronic Arts (EA). It is EA's longest-running **franchise**. It is also one of the most popular sports titles on the market. Some say *Madden NFL* is the most powerful franchise in North America!

Today's *Madden* titles offer gamers detailed, lifelike football experiences. Beyond facing off in matches, gamers can hire staff and trade players. They can even design their own stadiums!

Each year, a new *Madden NFL* rings in the football season. Every week, developers **update** more than

HALL OF FAMER

In August 2003, the *Madden* franchise entered the Pro Football Hall of Fame. It was the first video game ever featured in any pro sports hall of fame!

With the release of *Madden NFL 19* in August 2018, the number of *Madden* players hit 200 million.

400 player ratings to match the latest National Football League (NFL) **statistics**. To many, the **franchise** is simply known as *Madden*. Others consider it the "33rd team" of the NFL!

THE LONG GAME

Madden NFL began with a boy named William Murray "Trip" Hawkins III. The future EA founder fell in love with sports and **strategy** games as a child. In 1967, 14-year-old Trip discovered Strat-O-Matic Baseball. The tabletop sports **simulator** brought his favorite things together! But its football version disappointed him. Trip knew he could make something better.

As a student at Harvard University, Hawkins created Accu-Stat Football. This tabletop strategy game required a lot of math. It was too **complex** for everyday gamers.

The answer came to Hawkins in 1975. If Accu-Stat were a computer game, it could do the math itself. This would make the game more appealing to more people. Hawkins decided he would create his own computer game company.

After graduating college in 1976, Hawkins studied business at Stanford University. Two years later, he began working at Apple Computers in Cupertino, California. He directed Apple's

Hawkins' college degree was called "strategy and applied game theory." But he calls it "the world's first degree in games"!

marketing. While at the company, Hawkins learned all he could about business and technology.

Hawkins left Apple in 1982. The world was ready for his dream company. That May, Electronic Arts was born.

EA rolled out its first games in 1983. But Hawkins' big goal was still in the works. That year, he hired programmer Robin Antonick to create a football **simulator** for the Apple II and other home computers.

Creating the simulator was hard work. The Apple II had little memory and storage. Developers used seven-player teams to keep the gameplay smooth and simple.

Hawkins wanted a football hero to represent the game. In 1984, he asked famous football coach and announcer John Madden to join the team. Madden was interested. But he had one condition. The game had to be true NFL football. And that meant 11-player teams.

The developers struggled to make this happen. A failed partnership with developer Bethesda Softworks caused more delays. But *John Madden Football* finally launched in June 1988.

As an NFL announcer, John Madden would draw over instant replays using a device called a telestrator.

Its Quick mode offered a simple balance of action and **strategy**. In Standard mode, gamers could edit teams and design plays.

The game's 11-on-11 approach was fresh, but its sales were modest. The blocky players were slow, and the playbook was **complex**. Competing titles, such as Cinemaware's *TV Sports: Football*, stole the spotlight.

A TALE OF TWO TITLES

By 1989, EA was ready for a rematch. Sega Games Company was creating the Genesis **console**. EA hired Park Place Productions to create a football game for it. Park Place filmed live football players to keep plays realistic. In six months, the new and improved *John Madden Football* was complete.

Meanwhile, Sega was developing a competing title, *Joe Montana Football*. But its producers were behind. So, Sega asked EA to help finish the game. EA didn't want to help a rival product. But, Sega threatened to delay the Genesis release.

EA could not take the risk. It had too many Genesis titles in development. So, EA had Park Place complete *Joe Montana*.

In December 1990, *John Madden Football* launched on the Sega Genesis and the new Super Nintendo Entertainment System (SNES). The first 40,000 *John Madden Football* games sold out in one afternoon! *Joe Montana Football* dropped one month later. But *John Madden Football* was the fan favorite.

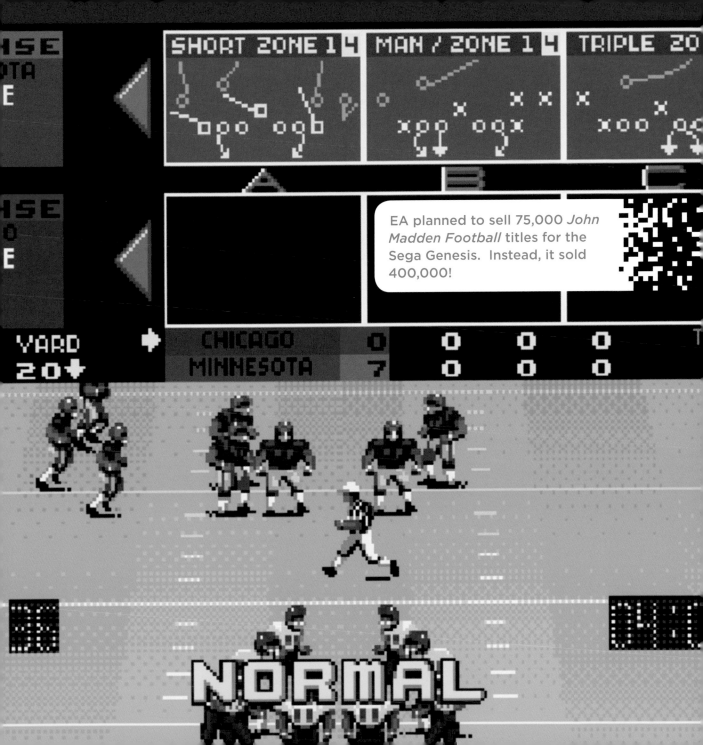

EA planned to sell 75,000 *John Madden Football* titles for the Sega Genesis. Instead, it sold 400,000!

RAGING RIVALRY

John Madden Football was a hit, but there was plenty of room to improve. *John Madden Football '92* was released in 1991 with instant replays and new formations. Gamers loved it! That year, EA created EA Sports to manage its sports titles.

EA Sports dropped *John Madden Football '93* in 1992. But this time, Sega stole the show. *NFL Sports Talk Football '93* was allowed to use NFL team names and logos. Meanwhile, *John Madden Football* was stuck with city names and plain colors.

EA acted fast. In 1993, it struck its own NFL deal. The next *Madden* game dropped in November with a new series name. *Madden NFL '94* featured official names and logos for all NFL teams! The next year, EA worked to include real NFL player names in *Madden NFL 95*. *Madden* was feeling like the real deal!

In 1995, EA Sports hosted the first *Madden* Bowl in Florida. Celebrities and NFL players competed in a *Madden* tournament for charity. Also in 1995, EA hired the developer Visual Concepts

In *Madden NFL '94*, players could choose from 80 different teams and 72 new offensive plays.

Packers
captain call it
in the air

to reinvent *Madden* for Sony's upcoming PlayStation **console**. But development fell far behind. Eventually, EA hired developer Tiburon Entertainment to create *Madden NFL 96* for the Genesis and SNES.

Madden NFL 96 dropped in November 1995. It was not a PlayStation title. But it did offer new plays, new **animations**, and player trading.

Meanwhile, the **franchise** rivalry raged on. Tiburon released *Madden NFL 97* with smooth **graphics** and **3-D** stadiums. But, Sony's *NFL GameDay* offered better **artificial intelligence (AI)**.

Its athletes had smoother, smarter moves. Tiburon improved its own AI for *Madden NFL 98*. Meanwhile, the new *GameDay* came in full 3-D. *Madden* remained a step behind the competition.

In 1998, EA made Tiburon the official *Madden* developer. *Madden NFL 99* dropped that July with full 3-D

COVER CURSE

Garrison Hearst of the San Francisco 49ers starred on the *Madden NFL 99* cover. Soon after, he broke his ankle, and the "Madden Curse" was born. Many *Madden* cover athletes have been injured or played poorly after the game's release!

Steven Chiang helped start Tiburon Entertainment in 1994. Tiburon was acquired by EA in 1998.

graphics and a new **Franchise** mode. As NFL general managers, players could select, trade, and substitute players over 15 seasons!

Madden NFL 2000's fast, smooth gameplay kept the ball rolling. Sega fought back with *NFL 2K* for its new Dreamcast **console**. But EA was still in the game. When *Madden NFL 2001* launched on the new PlayStation 2, its graphics and **AI** crushed the competition.

THE LEAGUE'S CHOICE

The battle of the game developers continued. In August 2002, *Madden NFL 2003* introduced EA's first online play mode. Then in 2003, Sega partnered with ESPN to match the look of TV sports in *ESPN NFL Football*. That August, *Madden NFL 2004* revealed the most detailed gameplay yet. Its **Franchise** mode let players organize practices, hire coaches, and more.

Sega upped the competition. In 2004, *ESPN NFL 2K5* dropped one month earlier than *Madden NFL 2005*, and at half the price. Still, *Madden NFL 2005* was a fan favorite. Its Hit Stick feature allowed better tackle control. And the new "EA Sports Radio" show brought player stories to life.

In December, EA announced a new NFL contract. *Madden* was officially the only series allowed to feature NFL teams, stadiums, and players. It was a true franchise touchdown!

In August 2005, *Madden NFL 06* launched on Microsoft's new Xbox 360 **console**. It introduced Superstar mode. In this

In December 2005, ESPN introduced the reality TV show *Madden Nation*. It followed top *Madden* gamers competing in tournaments across the country.

single-player mode, gamers could play through the career of a new NFL player. Reviews were mixed. Critics worried the quality of the **franchise** was suffering. Now that *Madden* was the only NFL video game, it faced no pressure to be the best.

GAME CHANGERS

EA stepped up its game with *Madden NFL 07* in August 2006. It sold more than 3.9 million copies, making it the best-selling game of 2006. *Madden NFL 08* introduced smoother gameplay and better passing controls.

Madden NFL 09 **debuted** at college football's Rose Bowl in August 2008. There, EA celebrated 20 years of the **franchise**. *Madden NFL 09* introduced online league play. Now, gamers could play through an entire NFL season in online groups of up to 32 players. It was a best-selling game of 2008.

Each *Madden* release brought new twists. In *Madden* Ultimate Team mode, gamers could build their own online teams by purchasing and swapping player trading cards. The GameFlow feature let casual gamers have plays called for them. Meanwhile, hardcore players could create their own plays.

Over the coming years, *Madden* developers struggled to keep up with new **consoles** and technology. Fans complained

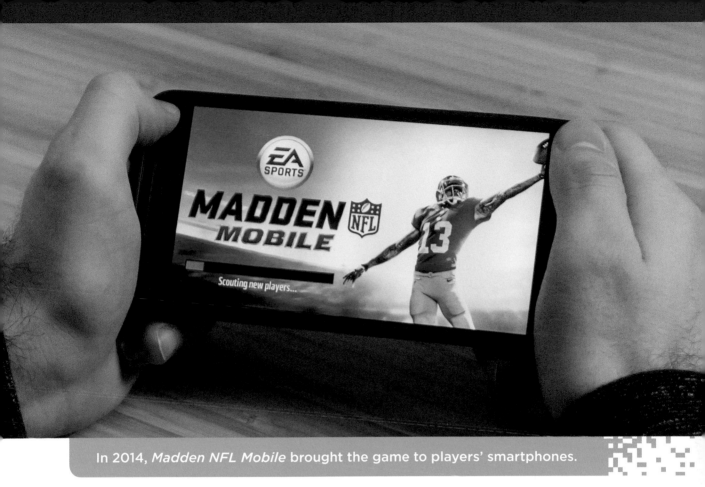

In 2014, *Madden NFL Mobile* brought the game to players' smartphones.

the games felt tired and unfinished. In 2011, Cam Weber stepped in as head of EA Sports. He and the development team worked to turn the **franchise** around.

In 2013, EA celebrated 25 years of *Madden* with *Madden NFL 25*. Its impressive **updates** shined on the new PlayStation 4 and Xbox One **consoles**.

7

CAPTURE THE ACTION

Animators bring *Madden*'s gameplay to life. However, live athletes and motion-capture technology play a big role in the animation process.

Developers record new *Madden* footage at The Capture Lab in Vancouver, Canada. Motion-capture athletes (MCAs) help capture the latest NFL trends. Many MCAs are former college or pro football players.

MCAs suit up in full football gear. Developers then cover the MCAs with rubber markers. After warming up, the MCAs perform blocks and tackles all day long.

While filming, The Capture Lab is lit in red. The markers on the MCAs reflect that light, which bounces into the studio's cameras. Together, the cameras create a digital model of the reflected points. Animators connect those dots to form **3-D** player "skeletons." Then, animators model the skeletons to look like actual NFL players!

KEEP IT REAL

Madden MCAs do more than blocks and tackles. They also act out celebration dances, stretches, and other actions NFL players do between plays.

At The Capture Lab, more than 150 cameras work together to build the stars that will appear in *Madden* games.

8

THE CHAMPION-MAKER

By 2016, a new type of athlete was on the rise. Competitive, organized gaming was growing more popular than ever. In June, EA chief Peter Moore announced the *Madden* Championship Series (MCS). Every year, gamers could compete online to get into one of three live tournaments. Top players from the Classic, Club Championship, and Challenge tournaments would then compete at a *Madden* Bowl.

Madden was shaping upcoming athletes, too. High school football coaches were using the game to teach their teams **strategy**. In college football, younger players were seeing more success as quarterbacks. New NFL players needed less guidance.

In August 2017, *Madden NFL 18* **debuted** the first story mode of the

#WEAREMADDEN

Tragedy shook the *Madden* community on August 26, 2018. That day, two respected pro gamers were killed in a shooting at a Florida MCS event. *Madden* players supported one another on social media with the hashtag #WeAreMadden.

Madden NFL 19 introduced "Real Player Motion." This new animation technology made player movements more realistic than ever before.

series. In Longshot, players followed a high-school quarterback through his journey to the NFL. The next August, *Madden NFL 19* dropped. That month, EA's total *Madden* sales hit 130 million units!

LEVEL UP!

Madden NFL: Thirty Years and Counting

Madden NFL has come a long way from simple throwing, running, and tackling. New details and improvements keep fans coming back for more. "They add little things every year to make it more realistic," says **marketing** vice president Chip Lange.

1988

JOHN MADDEN FOOTBALL

+ Platforms: Commodore 64 and 128, Apple II, and MS-DOS home computers

+ **Graphics**: **2-D**

+ Modes: Quick, Standard

+ Single games only

+ **Generic** teams and players

+ Offline play only

+ Soundtrack: original music

MADDEN NFL 19

+ Platforms: Windows and Mac OS computers; PlayStation 4; Xbox One

+ **Graphics**: **3-D**; motion-capture **animation**

+ Modes: **Franchise**, Longshot, Madden Ultimate Team

+ Single games and seasonal play

+ NFL teams and players

+ Online or offline play

+ Soundtrack: rap and hip-hop hits; monthly music **updates**

CHECK THE NUMBERS

Madden uses a 100-point scale to rank every NFL player's skill level in speed, strength, and other categories. EA uses scout feedback, sports reports, and online data to update the rankings every week. And with each title release, pro NFL players race to check their game ratings.

9

THE 33RD TEAM

In recent years, *Madden* has mirrored real football more than ever. This has earned the game a respected place in **e-sports**.

In March 2019, EA opened the EA Broadcast Studio in Redwood City, California. The studio would host and broadcast all EA e-sports competitions. Its first event was the MCS Challenge tournament in March. In April, the studio hosted the *Madden* Bowl. The event drew more than 2 million online views!

In August, *Madden NFL 20* dropped. Its new Scenario Engine created weekly storylines based on player performance. The title also provided 140 special abilities through its Superstar X-Factor feature. This tool allowed gamers to select NFL players based on their real-life skills.

Madden NFL 20 might be the last yearly *Madden* title. **CEO** Andrew Wilson says better technology may allow for year-round **updates** instead. No matter what the future holds, the NFL's 33rd team has made sports and video game history!

Patrick Mahomes of the Kansas City Chiefs starred on the *Madden NFL 20* cover. The 23-year-old quarterback was the third-youngest cover athlete in *Madden* history.

TIMELINE

1984

John Madden agrees to work on EA's upcoming football video game.

1990

EA releases *John Madden Football* for the Sega Genesis.

1982

Trip Hawkins starts Electronic Arts.

1988

EA releases *John Madden Football* for the Apple II.

1995

EA Sports hosts the first *Madden* Bowl in Florida.

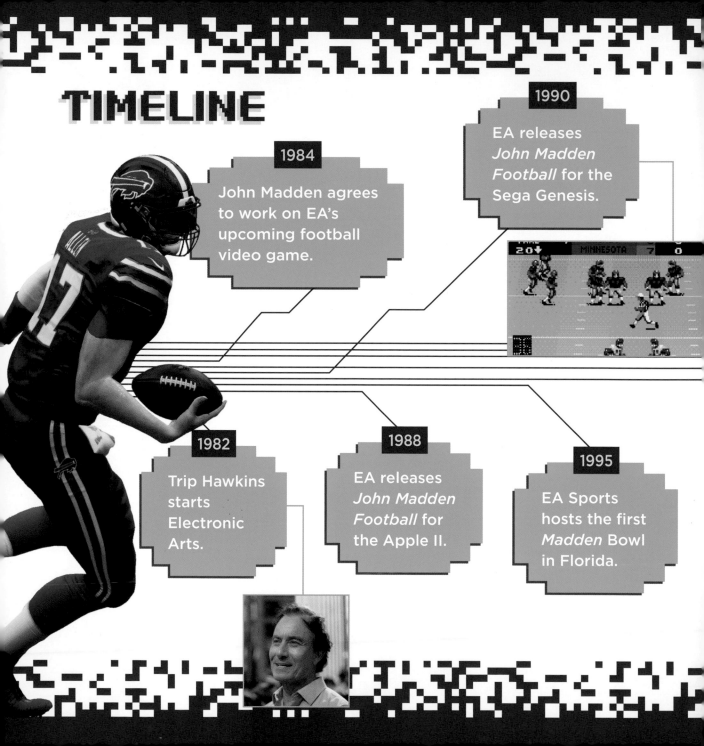

2004

EA announces a contract making *Madden* the only series allowed to feature NFL teams, stadiums, and players.

2016

EA announces the new *Madden* Championship Series.

2019

The EA Broadcast Studio opens in March. *Madden NFL 20* is released in August.

2008

EA debuts *Madden NFL 09* and celebrates 20 years of the franchise at the Rose Bowl.

2018

Madden NFL 19 drops in August. That month, total *Madden* sales hit 130 million units.

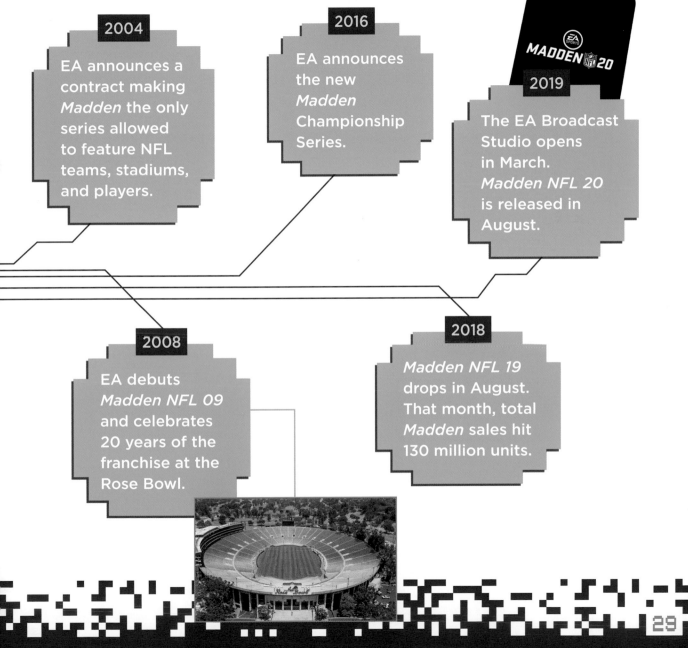

GLOSSARY

animation—a series of drawings, computer graphics, or photographs that appear to move due to slight changes in each image. An animator is a person who creates animations. To create animations is to animate.

artificial intelligence (AI)—the ability of a computer to imitate intelligent human behavior.

CEO—chief executive officer. The person who makes the major decisions for running an organization or business.

complex—having many parts, details, ideas, or functions.

console—an electronic system used to play video games.

debut (DAY-byoo)—to first appear.

e-sports—competitive, organized video gaming. *E-sports* stands for "electronic sports."

franchise—a series of related works, such as movies or video games, that feature the same characters. A franchise is also a team and its commercial operations within a professional sports league.

generic—having a general or common name as opposed to a specific one.

graphics—images on the screen of a computer, TV, or other device.

marketing—the process of advertising or promoting something so people will want to buy it.

simulation—something that is made to look, feel, or behave like something else. A simulator is a device that creates simulations.

statistics—also called stats. Numbers that represent pieces of information about a game or player.

strategy—a careful plan or method.

3-D—having length, width, and depth, or appearing to have these dimensions. *3-D* stands for "three-dimensional."

2-D—having length and width, but lacking the appearance of depth. *2-D* stands for "two-dimensional."

update—to make something more modern or up-to-date. An update is a more modern or up-to-date form of something.

ONLINE RESOURCES

Booklinks
NONFICTION NETWORK
FREE! ONLINE NONFICTION RESOURCES

To learn more about *Madden NFL*, please visit **abdobooklinks.com** or scan this QR code. These links are routinely monitored and updated to provide the most current information available.

INDEX